Tenor Sax

101 JAZZ SON

Note: The keys in this book do not match the other wind instruments.

Available for
FLUTE, CLARINET, ALTO SAX, TENOR SAX, TRUMPET,
HORN, TROMBONE, VIOLIN, VIOLA, CELLO

ISBN 978-1-4950-2340-8

HAL•LEONARD®

Visit Hal Leonard Online at **www.halleonard.com**

Explore the entire family of Hal Leonard products and resources

 SHEET MUSIC DIRECT SheetMusicPlus  HAL LEONARD'S ESSENTIAL ELEMENTS **music class**  **ESSENTIAL ELEMENTS** *Interactive*

 ArrangeMe noteflight groove3 musicroom

World headquarters, contact:
Hal Leonard
7777 West Bluemound Road
Milwaukee, WI 53213
Email: info@halleonard.com

In Europe, contact:
Hal Leonard Europe Limited
Dettingen Way
Bury St. Edmunds, Suffolk, IP33 3YB
Email: info@halleonardeurope.com

In Australia, contact:
Hal Leonard Australia Pty. Ltd.
4 Lentara Court
Cheltenham, Victoria, 3192 Australia
Email: info@halleonard.com.au

CONTENTS

ALL OF ME

TENOR SAX

Words and Music by SEYMOUR SIMONS
and GERALD MARKS

Moderately

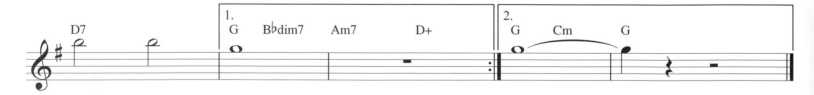

ALL THE THINGS YOU ARE

TENOR SAX

Lyrics by OSCAR HAMMERSTEIN II
Music by JEROME KERN

APRIL IN PARIS

TENOR SAX

Words by E.Y. "YIP" HARBURG
Music by VERNON DUKE

Moderately

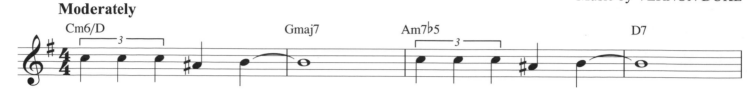

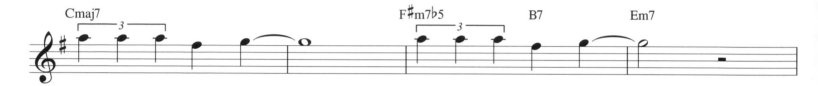

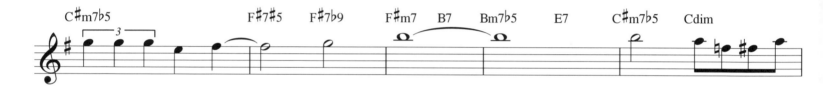

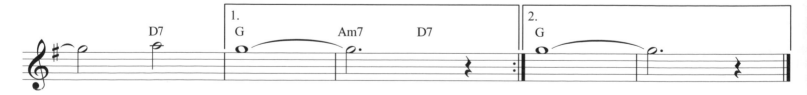

AUTUMN IN NEW YORK

TENOR SAX

Words and Music by
VERNON DUKE

AUTUMN LEAVES

TENOR SAX

English Lyric by JOHNNY MERCER
French Lyric by JACQUES PREVERT
Music by JOSEPH KOSMA

BEWITCHED

TENOR SAX

Words by LORENZ HART
Music by RICHARD RODGERS

BEYOND THE SEA

Lyrics by JACK LAWRENCE
Music by CHARLES TRENET and ALBERT LASRY
Original French Lyric to "La Mer" by CHARLES TRENET

TENOR SAX

THE BLUE ROOM

TENOR SAX

Words by LORENZ HART
Music by RICHARD RODGERS

BLUE SKIES

TENOR SAX

Words and Music by
IRVING BERLIN

BLUESETTE

TENOR SAX

Words by NORMAN GIMBEL
Music by JEAN THIELEMANS

BODY AND SOUL

TENOR SAX

Words by EDWARD HEYMAN,
ROBERT SOUR and FRANK EYTON
Music by JOHN GREEN

BUT BEAUTIFUL

TENOR SAX

Words by JOHNNY BURKE
Music by JIMMY VAN HEUSEN

CAN'T HELP LOVIN' DAT MAN

TENOR SAX

Lyrics by OSCAR HAMMERSTEIN II
Music by JEROME KERN

Moderately and rather freely, with a lilt

CARAVAN

TENOR SAX

Words and Music by DUKE ELLINGTON,
IRVING MILLS and JUAN TIZOL

CHARADE

TENOR SAX

By HENRY MANCINI

CHEEK TO CHEEK

TENOR SAX

Words and Music by
IRVING BERLIN

COME RAIN OR COME SHINE

TENOR SAX

Words by JOHNNY MERCER
Music by HAROLD ARLEN

Moderately slow

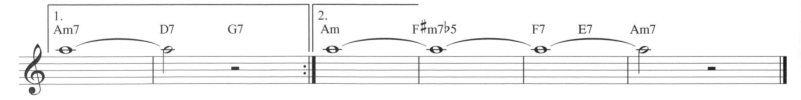

DANCING ON THE CEILING

TENOR SAX

Words by LORENZ HART
Music by RICHARD RODGERS

DEARLY BELOVED

TENOR SAX

Music by JEROME KERN
Words by JOHNNY MERCER

DO NOTHIN' TILL YOU HEAR FROM ME

TENOR SAX

Words and Music by DUKE ELLINGTON
and BOB RUSSELL

DON'T GET AROUND MUCH ANYMORE

TENOR SAX

Words and Music by DUKE ELLINGTON
and BOB RUSSELL

DREAMSVILLE

Tenor Sax

By HENRY MANCINI

FALLING IN LOVE WITH LOVE

TENOR SAX

Words by LORENZ HART
Music by RICHARD RODGERS

A FINE ROMANCE

Tenor Sax

Words by DOROTHY FIELDS
Music by JEROME KERN

FLY ME TO THE MOON
(In Other Words)

TENOR SAX

Words and Music by
BART HOWARD

Moderately

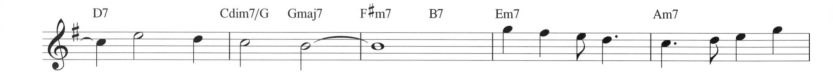

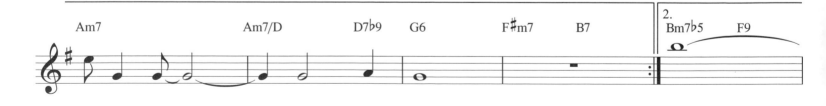

GEORGIA ON MY MIND

TENOR SAX

Words by STUART GORRELL
Music by HOAGY CARMICHAEL

HERE'S THAT RAINY DAY

TENOR SAX

Words by JOHNNY BURKE
Music by JIMMY VAN HEUSEN

HERE'S TO LIFE

TENOR SAX

Music by ARTIE BUTLER
Lyrics by PHYLLIS MOLINARY

HONEYSUCKLE ROSE

TENOR SAX

Words by ANDY RAZAF
Music by THOMAS "FATS" WALLER

HOW DEEP IS THE OCEAN
(How High Is the Sky)

TENOR SAX

Words and Music by
IRVING BERLIN

HOW INSENSITIVE
(Insensatez)

TENOR SAX

Music by ANTONIO CARLOS JOBIM
Original Words by VINICIUS DE MORAES
English Words by NORMAN GIMBEL

Medium Bossa Nova

I CAN'T GET STARTED

TENOR SAX

Words by IRA GERSHWIN
Music by VERNON DUKE

I COULD WRITE A BOOK

TENOR SAX

Words by LORENZ HART
Music by RICHARD RODGERS

I GOT IT BAD AND THAT AIN'T GOOD

TENOR SAX

Words by PAUL FRANCIS WEBSTER
Music by DUKE ELLINGTON

I'LL REMEMBER APRIL

TENOR SAX

Words and Music by PAT JOHNSTON,
DON RAYE AND GENE DE PAUL

Moderately

I'M BEGINNING TO SEE THE LIGHT

TENOR SAX

Words and Music by DON GEORGE, JOHNNY HODGES,
DUKE ELLINGTON and HARRY JAMES

Medium Bounce

I'VE GOT THE WORLD ON A STRING

TENOR SAX

Words by TED KOEHLER
Music by HAROLD ARLEN

IF I WERE A BELL

TENOR SAX

By FRANK LOESSER

Bright Swing

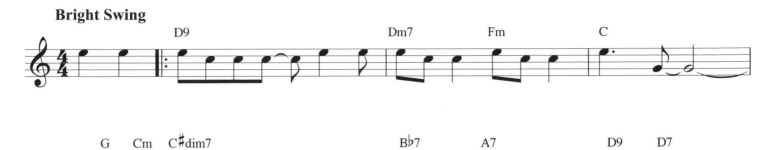

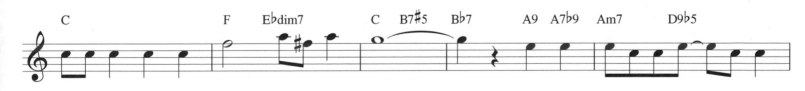

IMAGINATION

TENOR SAX

Words by JOHNNY BURKE
Music by JIMMY VAN HEUSEN

IN A SENTIMEMTAL MOOD

TENOR SAX

By DUKE ELLINGTON

IN THE WEE SMALL HOURS OF THE MORNING

TENOR SAX

Words by BOB HILLIARD
Music by DAVID MANN

INDIANA
(Back Home Again in Indiana)

TENOR SAX

Words by BALLARD MacDONALD
Music by JAMES F. HANLEY

ISN'T IT ROMANTIC?

TENOR SAX

Words by LORENZ HART
Music by RICHARD RODGERS

IT COULD HAPPEN TO YOU

TENOR SAX

Words by JOHNNY BURKE
Music by JAMES VAN HEUSEN

IT DON'T MEAN A THING
(If It Ain't Got That Swing)

Tenor Sax

Words and Music by DUKE ELLINGTON
and IRVING MILLS

Fast Swing

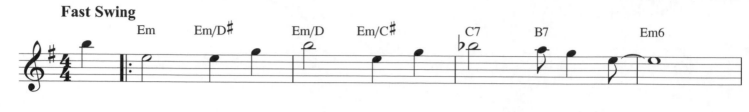

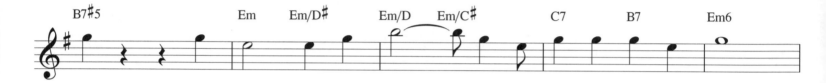

IT MIGHT AS WELL BE SPRING

TENOR SAX

Lyrics by OSCAR HAMMERSTEIN II
Music by RICHARD RODGERS

Moderately

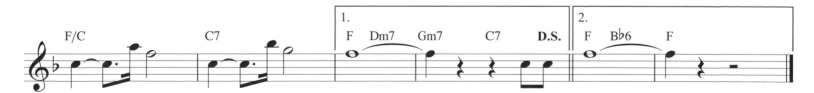

THE LADY IS A TRAMP

TENOR SAX

Words by LORENZ HART
Music by RICHARD RODGERS

LAZY RIVER

TENOR SAX

Words and Music by HOAGY CARMICHAEL
and SIDNEY ARODIN

LET THERE BE LOVE

TENOR SAX

Lyric by IAN GRANT
Music by LIONEL RAND

LIKE SOMEONE IN LOVE

TENOR SAX

Words by JOHNNY BURKE
Music by JIMMY VAN HEUSEN

LITTLE GIRL BLUE

Tenor Sax

Words by LORENZ HART
Music by RICHARD RODGERS

Long Ago (And Far Away)

TENOR SAX

Words by IRA GERSHWIN
Music by JEROME KERN

LOVER, COME BACK TO ME

TENOR SAX

Lyrics by OSCAR HAMMERSTEIN II
Music by SIGMUND ROMBERG

Moderately

LULLABY OF BIRDLAND

TENOR SAX

Words by GEORGE DAVID WEISS
Music by GEORGE SHEARING

Moderate Swing

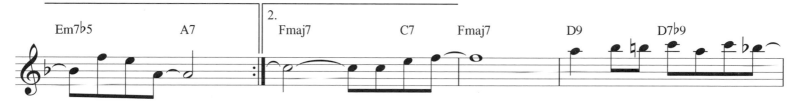

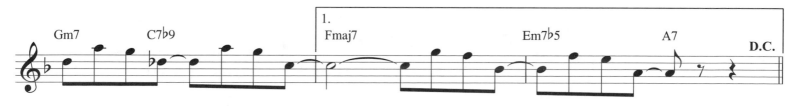

LULLABY OF THE LEAVES

TENOR SAX

Words by JOE YOUNG
Music by BERNICE PETKERE

MANHATTAN

TENOR SAX

Words by LORENZ HART
Music by RICHARD RODGERS

MEDITATION
(Meditação)

TENOR SAX

Music by ANTONIO CARLOS JOBIM
Original Words by NEWTON MENDONÇA
English Words by NORMAN GIMBEL

Medium Bossa Nova

MIDNIGHT SUN

TENOR SAX

Words and Music by LIONEL HAMPTON,
SONNY BURKE and JOHNNY MERCER

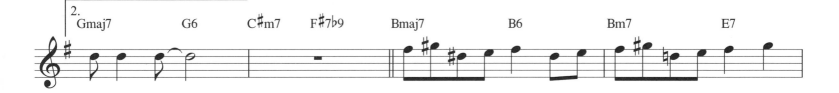

MISTY

TENOR SAX

Music by ERROLL GARNER

MOOD INDIGO

TENOR SAX

Words and Music by DUKE ELLINGTON,
IRVING MILLS and ALBANY BIGARD

MOONLIGHT IN VERMONT

TENOR SAX

Words by JOHN BLACKBURN
Music by KARL SUESSDORF

MORE THAN YOU KNOW

TENOR SAX

Words by WILLIAM ROSE and EDWARD ELISCU
Music by VINCENT YOUMANS

MY HEART STOOD STILL

TENOR SAX

Words by LORENZ HART
Music by RICHARD RODGERS

MY OLD FLAME

TENOR SAX

Words and Music by ARTHUR JOHNSTON
and SAM COSLOW

Moderate Swing

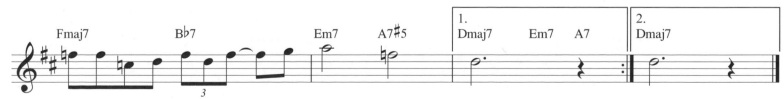

MY ONE AND ONLY LOVE

TENOR SAX

Words by ROBERT MELLIN
Music by GUY WOOD

MY ROMANCE

TENOR SAX

Words by LORENZ HART
Music by RICHARD RODGERS

MY SHIP

TENOR SAX

Words by IRA GERSHWIN
Music by KURT WEILL

THE NEARNESS OF YOU

TENOR SAX

Words by NED WASHINGTON
Music by HOAGY CARMICHAEL

A NIGHT IN TUNISIA

TENOR SAX

By JOHN "DIZZY" GILLESPIE
and FRANK PAPARELLI

Moderately fast Swing

ON GREEN DOLPHIN STREET

TENOR SAX

Lyrics by NED WASHINGTON
Music by BRONISLAU KAPER

ONE NOTE SAMBA
(Samba de uma nota so)

TENOR SAX

Original Lyrics by NEWTON MENDONÇA
English Lyrics by ANTONIO CARLOS JOBIM
Music by ANTONIO CARLOS JOBIM

Medium Bossa Nova

PICK YOURSELF UP

TENOR SAX

Words by DOROTHY FIELDS
Music by JEROME KERN

POLKA DOTS AND MOONBEAMS

TENOR SAX

Words by JOHNNY BURKE
Music by JIMMY VAN HEUSEN

QUIET NIGHTS OF QUIET STARS
(Corcovado)

Tenor Sax

English Words by GENE LEES
Original Words and Music by ANTONIO CARLOS JOBIM

Medium Bossa Nova

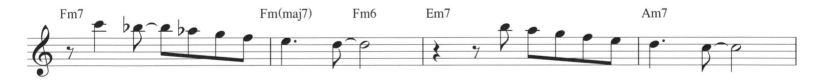

SATIN DOLL

TENOR SAX

By DUKE ELLINGTON

SKYLARK

TENOR SAX

Words by JOHNNY MERCER
Music by HOAGY CARMICHAEL

Moderate Swing

SO NICE
(Summer Samba)

TENOR SAX

Original Words and Music by MARCOS VALLE
and PAULO SERGIO VALLE
English Words by NORMAN GIMBEL

Medium Bossa Nova

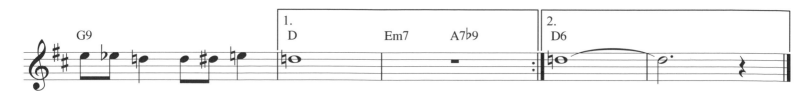

SOPHISTICATED LADY

TENOR SAX

Words and Music by DUKE ELLINGTON,
IRVING MILLS and MITCHELL PARISH

Moderately

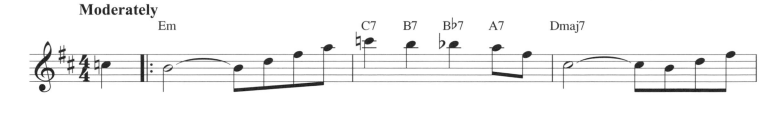

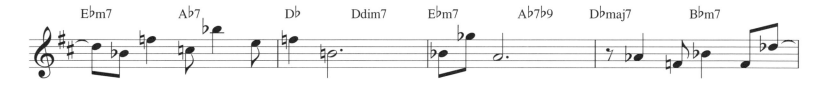

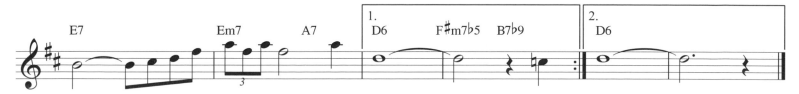

SPEAK LOW

TENOR SAX

Words by OGDEN NASH
Music by KURT WEILL

Moderately

STELLA BY STARLIGHT

Tenor Sax

Words by NED WASHINGTON
Music by VICTOR YOUNG

STOMPIN' AT THE SAVOY

TENOR SAX

By BENNY GOODMAN,
EDGAR SAMPSON and CHICK WEBB

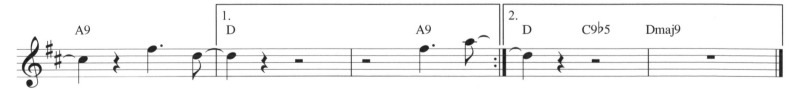

STORMY WEATHER
(Keeps Rainin' All the Time)

TENOR SAX

Lyric by TED KOEHLER
Music by HAROLD ARLEN

A Sunday Kind of Love

TENOR SAX

Words and Music by LOUIS PRIMA, ANITA NYE LEONARD,
STANLEY RHODES and BARBARA BELLE

Tangerine

TENOR SAX

Words by JOHNNY MERCER
Music by VICTOR SCHERTZINGER

THERE'S A SMALL HOTEL

TENOR SAX

Words by LORENZ HART
Music by RICHARD RODGERS

THESE FOOLISH THINGS (REMIND ME OF YOU)

TENOR SAX

Words by HOLT MARVELL
Music by JACK STRACHEY

THE THINGS WE DID LAST SUMMER

TENOR SAX

Words by SAMMY CAHN
Music by JULE STYNE

THIS CAN'T BE LOVE

TENOR SAX

Words by LORENZ HART
Music by RICHARD RODGERS

Moderately

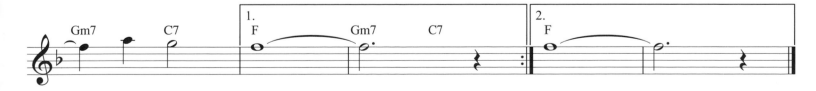

THOU SWELL

TENOR SAX

Words by LORENZ HART
Music by RICHARD RODGERS

Moderately

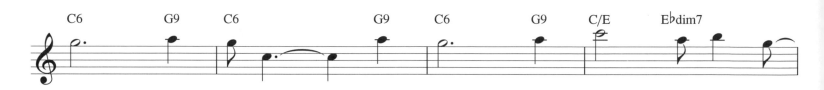

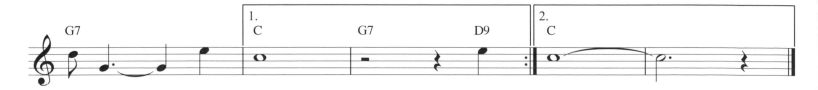

UNFORGETTABLE

TENOR SAX

Words and Music by
IRVING GORDON

THE VERY THOUGHT OF YOU

TENOR SAX

Words and Music by
RAY NOBLE

WATCH WHAT HAPPENS

Tenor Sax

Music by MICHEL LEGRAND
Original French Text by JACQUES DEMY
English Lyrics by NORMAN GIMBEL

WAVE

TENOR SAX

Words and Music by
ANTONIO CARLOS JOBIM

Medium Bossa Nova

THE WAY YOU LOOK TONIGHT

Tenor Sax

Words by DOROTHY FIELDS
Music by JEROME KERN

WHAT'LL I DO

TENOR SAX

Words and Music by
IRVING BERLIN

WILLOW WEEP FOR ME

TENOR SAX

Words and Music by
ANN RONELL

WITCHCRAFT

TENOR SAX

Music by CY COLEMAN
Lyrics by CAROLYN LEIGH

Moderately

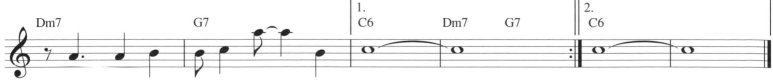

YESTERDAYS

TENOR SAX

Words by OTTO HARBACH
Music by JEROME KERN

YOU ARE TOO BEAUTIFUL

TENOR SAX

Words by LORENZ HART
Music by RICHARD RODGERS

YOU BROUGHT A NEW KIND OF LOVE TO ME

TENOR SAX

Words and Music by SAMMY FAIN,
IRVING KAHAL and PIERRE NORMAN

Medium Swing

YOU DON'T KNOW WHAT LOVE IS

TENOR SAX

Words and Music by DON RAYE
and GENE DePAUL